"I saw a child fall down. Under a shower of bullets, I rushed forward and went for the picture. It had been a peaceful march, the children were told to disperse, they started singing 'Nkosi Sikelele.' The police were ordered to shoot."

Sam Nzima, photojournalist

*For Dorothy Molefi and all mothers
who have buried their children.*

For courageous Antoinette Sithole and Sam Nzima.

And for Adam, Sophia, Greg, and Claire, with love.

First published in 2019 by Page Street Kids,
an imprint of
Page Street Publishing Co.
27 Congress Street, Suite 105
Salem, MA 01970
www.pagestreetpublishing.com

Distributed by Macmillan, sales in Canada by The Canadian Manda Group

19 20 21 22 23 CCO   5 4 3 2 1

ISBN-13: 978-1-62414-691-6
ISBN-10: 1-624-14691-0

CIP data for this book is available from the Library of Congress.

This book was typeset in Iowan Old Style.
The illustrations were done in pastel and collage.
Printed and bound in Shenzhen, Guangdong, China

Page Street Publishing uses only materials from suppliers who are committed to
responsible and sustainable forest management.

Page Street Publishing protects our planet by donating to nonprofits like The Trustees,
which focuses on local land conservation.

HECTOR

A Boy, a Protest, and the Photograph that Changed Apartheid

Adrienne Wright

PAGE
STREET
KIDS

South Africa was first colonized by Dutch and British settlers in between the 1600s and 1800s. Descendants of the Dutch settlers spoke Afrikaans, a language derived mainly from Dutch. Discrimination and segregation were part of society, but in 1948, they became a law called *apartheid*. Just when many countries were abandoning segregation, South Africa began enforcing it. People were required to live in areas segregated by race, and many black people were moved to townships outside of cities. One of the largest townships was Soweto (SOuth-WEstern TOwnships), on the south-western outskirts of Johannesburg.

The government spent less on education for black students than for whites. This inequality caused anger and frustration, and it worsened in the mid-1970s, when the government made a new law. Black students were required to learn half their subjects in Afrikaans. Until then, they were taught in English, which students preferred, because it was seen as an international language. Lessons in Afrikaans added hardship to students and teachers in an already oppressive education system. Black township students described Afrikaans as "the language of the oppressor."

On June 16, 1976, black high school student leaders in Soweto planned a peaceful protest of the new education law. Many younger students got caught up in the protest.

One of those younger students was Hector Zolile Pieterson.

HECTOR

Soweto, Saturday, June 12

Hector is an ordinary twelve-year-old boy. His weekends are filled with playing soccer, doing chores, watching his favorite movies, and visiting family.

When Hector hears Mma call his traditional name, he drags himself away from the game. It's time to head home.

After his regular chores, Hector offers to run errands for his neighbors to make some pocket money.

Cornmeal from the spaza, Hector.

Chuck meat and soup bones for me, please.

Back at home, he counts how much he's made. He'll use it to buy movie tickets and some candy.

One, two, three, four, five cents. Sharp-sharp!

Maybe you should practice counting in Afrikaans? That's how it's going to be in school now.

Sharp-sharp!

Een, twee, drie, vier, vyf . . .

On Saturday afternoons, Hector and his friends love watching movies at the nearby church.

He watches his hero, Bruce Lee, on the screen, who never disappoints.

On the way home, the boys reenact their favorite scenes from the movie. Hector keeps his friends entertained.

Sensei Hector says,

"Focus on your opponent."

"Your mind is your best weapon."

"Don't slip."

Granny Mma's house, Monday, June 14

After school on Monday, Hector is happy to see his sister at Granny Mma's house.

Granny Mma calls Hector in and gives him some money to take home to Mma.

On his way home, Hector cuts through the veld, the quickest way from Granny Mma's house. It's also his favorite playground, where he practices his Bruce Lee moves.

Out of nowhere, bullying tsotsis appear and grab the envelope of money. Hector wrestles it back from them and runs through the thorny blackjacks of the veld to escape.

He pulls himself together as he tries to shake off the unusual encounter.

Hector thinks about telling Mma about the tsotsis but decides he'd rather not worry her.

Mma gasps at the prickly sight of Hector.

Ai, Zolile! You're covered in blackjacks! You came through the veld again?

To save the bus fare, Mma!

Antoinette said she'll come and help you on Friday. She sends her love. Granny Mma too.

Soweto, Wednesday, June 16

The sun's not up yet, but Hector is. It's a day just like any other as he gets ready for school.

Mma, can I wear my long trousers today?

No. You know the school uniform is shorts.

But it's so cold outside! One day, we're going to have a bathroom inside. With a hot tap and a toilet.

You are always dreaming. Dreaming and joking. Tsamaya sentle, Zolile.

Sala sentle, Mma. Stay well.

The schools are open, but students aren't going in for classes. Hector and his friend are drawn to the sound of chanting and singing. Everybody is marching to Orlando Stadium to protest a new law requiring schools to teach half of their lessons in Afrikaans.

No more Afrikaans!

More students join in, and soon hundreds, then thousands of people are marching. Hector is swept up in the excited activity of the growing crowd.

When the first Hippo truck blocks the street, they come to a halt.

Not to be intimidated, the students turn and march down another street toward the stadium, waving signs. They sing the government-banned anthem, "Nkosi Sikelel' iAfrika"—"God Bless Africa." Hector soaks in the meaning of the beautiful song: *Hear our petitions. God bless us, your children.*

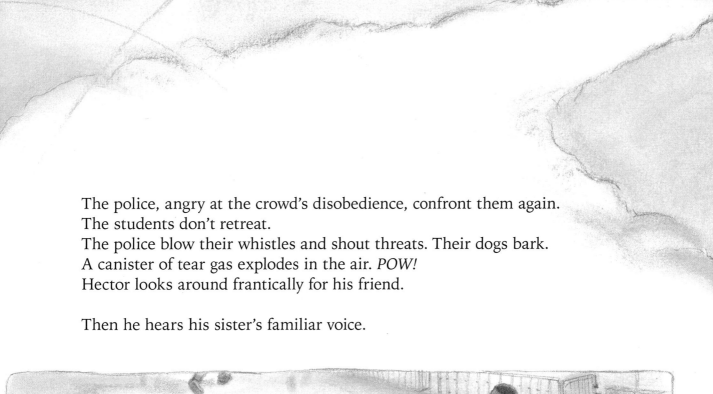

The police, angry at the crowd's disobedience, confront them again.
The students don't retreat.
The police blow their whistles and shout threats. Their dogs bark.
A canister of tear gas explodes in the air. *POW!*
Hector looks around frantically for his friend.

Then he hears his sister's familiar voice.

Hector!
You shouldn't be here!
We have to get you home.

Now!

ANTOINETTE

Granny Mma's house, Wednesday, June 16

The sun's not up yet, but Hector's older sister Antoinette is. She and some of her cousins stay with Granny Mma because her house is closer to their school. At least Mma can save train fare for one of her children.

Antoinette keeps the rumors about the protest to herself. She has a feeling there won't be any school today, but she takes her schoolbag anyway.

No need to worry Granny Mma.

Tsamaya sentle.

Sala sentle, Granny Mma.

At school, Antoinette finds a crowd gathering in the street, singing the banned anthem. Excited protesters arrive carrying signs and pepper the singing with shouts of their demands.

Nkosi sikele

NO MORE AFRIKAAN

AWAY WITH AFRIKAA

POW! Tear gas explodes in the air. Students scatter in all directions.

Then Antoinette spots Hector amidst the chaos.

Hector! You shouldn't be here!
We have to get you home.
Now!

But they're separated as they try to run for cover.

As the smoke clears, Antoinette sees a teenager bending over a child lying in the street. He gathers up the child in his arms and runs toward a car.

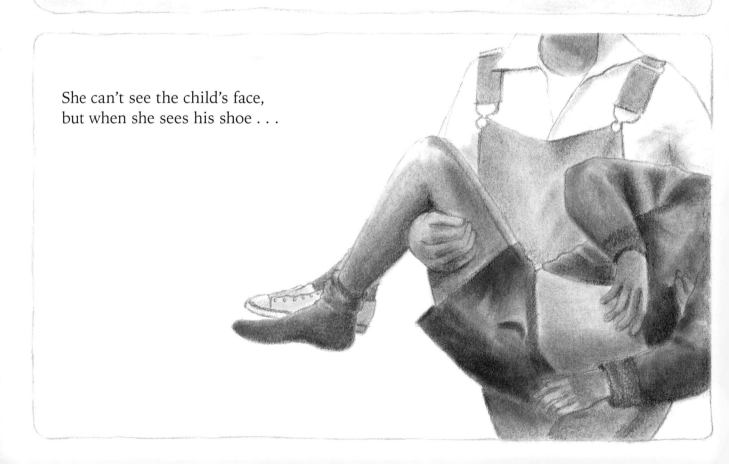

She can't see the child's face,
but when she sees his shoe . . .

RUN!

HELP!

My brother!

SAM

Soweto, Wednesday, June 16

The sun's not up yet, but photojournalist Sam Nzima is. He's already working, out on assignment for *The World* newspaper, covering the growing student protest.

The protest begins.
The students march.
Sam snaps photos.

The police arrive.
Their dogs bark.
Sam snaps photos.

The police barricades go up.
The children sing.
Sam snaps photos.

The police shoot!
Sam snaps.

Sam knows he's seen something important.

The police think so too. They destroy all the film they can find.

But Sam is one step ahead of the police. He's already hidden the most precious roll of film.

When he's safely away from the action, he sends the film back to the newspaper's office to be developed.

His photograph of Hector, Antoinette, and another student
runs on the front page of the newspaper.

That evening, *The World* lies on Granny Mma's kitchen table.
Hector never came home.

Nothing quite like this had ever happened before in South Africa.
Not to school children.

Not to an ordinary boy like Hector.

Hector lives on as a compelling symbol of the cost of apartheid
and the change sparked by students that day.

After the Photograph

The students never reached Orlando Stadium on June 16, 1976, but their spirit of protest spread throughout the region and the rest of the country. It will take fourteen more years for apartheid to be abolished. Sam's photograph became a powerful symbol, opening the world's eyes to the racism and violence of apartheid and provoking change in South Africa.

Many died on June 16, 1976, and in the following months in clashes with the police. The struggle against apartheid began in earnest after June 16, and the law requiring black students to learn subjects in Afrikaans was abandoned. In the early 1990s, apartheid ended, but its effects are still felt today.

The song "Nkosi Sikelel' iAfrika," originally a hymn, found new life as a liberation song in the fight to end apartheid. Although it was banned during apartheid, the song became South Africa's national anthem in 1994 and incorporated the previous white government's Afrikaans anthem, "Die Stem." Today's anthem includes five languages: Xhosa, Zulu, Sesotho, Afrikaans, and English.

June 16 is now a public holiday in South Africa known as "Youth Day" in remembrance of those who protested and those who died protesting apartheid. In 2002, the Hector Pieterson Memorial and Museum was built in Soweto "to honor the youth who gave their lives in the struggle for freedom and democracy."

Author's Note

Growing up white in South Africa, I saw the practices of apartheid and the police, but I was not subject to them. I knew of Sam's powerful photograph of Hector Pieterson and was surprised that no books had been written about Hector's story. Because there is no documented record of Hector's life, I invented dialogue to show his personality and routines based on stories his mother (Mma) Dorothy Molefi and sister Antoinette told me. Antoinette and Dorothy, both of whom I was fortunate to meet, graciously answered many questions about Hector and the events of June 16. Antoinette also gave me a tour of the museum, and Dorothy hosted me at her home, where Hector had lived. The scenes depict actual incidents that happened to Hector or reflect his usual daily life.

I am also grateful to have spoken with photographer Sam Nzima, who shared in detail what he witnessed and heard on June 16, as well as his life after that day.

The richly detailed, first-hand accounts of Hector's life and the events of June 16 by Dorothy Molefi, Antoinette Sithole, and Sam Nzima helped build a distinct picture of how I wanted to tell this story.

Hector Zolile Pieterson Hector's mother Dorothy Molefi often called him Zolile, his traditional name, meaning "calmness." She didn't know about the protests and only learned about her son's death when she returned home from work that evening. When she saw the photo of Hector on the front page of the newspaper, she thought he was wounded. After journalists borrowed family photographs that were never returned, that photo was the only one Dorothy had of her son until 2014, when a magazine found a photograph in their archive: Hector, dapper in a suit and hat, posing on his fourth birthday.

Antoinette Sithole Since Antoinette attended a different school than Hector and was living with her grandmother, Granny Mma, at the time, it was by chance that she found Hector at the protest. She is now an advocate for continuing Hector's legacy. She is a motivational speaker and occasionally leads tours for special groups and dignitaries at the museum. Antoinette named one of her sons Hector, after her brother.

Sam Nzima Sam's photograph of Hector was printed in newspapers across the country and around the world. However, Sam was threatened by the police, and his career as a photojournalist was over. He returned to his hometown, Lillydale, where he owned a store and taught photography. Decades later, Sam was finally given the copyright to his iconic photograph, but he is still not always credited when it is used. If not for Sam's quick thinking, hiding the roll of film in his sock, the cause of the students—and apartheid itself—might not have received the global attention it did. Sam died on May 12, 2018, at the age of 83.

Mbuyisa Makhubu The third person in the photo, Mbuyisa Makhubu, is the teenager who carried Hector out of the street. He said afterward that he could feel the "heaviness" of Hector and knew that he was already dead as he placed him in the car. After the photograph was published, eighteen-year-old Mbuyisa was harassed by police and went into exile. His mother last heard from him in 1978, when she received a letter from him postmarked from Nigeria, where he'd sought refuge.

Glossary

Afrikaans: language unique to southern Africa, derived mainly from Dutch

Apartheid: (*a-PART-hayt*; Afrikaans language) "apart-ness," segregation

Blackjacks: a weed with barbed seeds

Dumela: (*doo-MEH-la*; Sesotho language) hello

Heita: (*hay-TA*; Sesotho language, slang) hi

Hippo: armored vehicle originally used by the military, then used by police for crowd control

Mma: (Sesotho language) mother, when addressing her

"Nkosi Sikelel' iAfrika": (*nn-KOH-see see-keh-LEH-lee a-FREE-kah*) "God Bless Africa"; now the South African national anthem. In 1976, it was an unofficial, banned anthem, with three verses in South African languages: Xhosa, Zulu, and Sesotho.

Sala sentle / Tsamaya sentle: (*SAH-lah SEN-tleh / tsa-MY-ah SEN-tleh*; Setswana language) goodbye; "Go well," said to the person leaving / "Stay well," said to the person staying

Soweto: (*soh-WEH-toh*) abbreviation for SOuth-WEstern TOwnships; residential area designated for black South Africans on the outskirts of Johannesburg

Spaza: (*SPAH-zah*; township slang) unlicensed small shop, sometimes hidden within a home, selling basic everyday items such as matches, soap, paraffin, tea, and sugar

Tsotsi: (*TSOH-tsee*; Sesotho language, slang) pickpocket, township bully

Veld: (*FELT*; Afrikaans language) open grassland

Acknowledgments

Sincere thanks to Antoinette Sithole, for patiently answering endless questions about June 16 and her family; Dorothy Molefi, for sharing her heartbreaking story for the umpteenth time and for her remarkable strength; and Sam Nzima, for great courage in capturing the iconic photograph and allowing me to use it in this book.

To my family and friends, with thanks and love: daughter Sophia Bagg, wise beyond her years, whose opinions and poses were invaluable; husband Adam Bagg, for constant support, love, and patient poses; sister Claire Wright and brother Greg Wright, for unwavering support, counseling, and wisdom. To brother-in-law Graeme Simpson and friend Christine Woyshner, for advice and lengthy discussions. A special thank-you to Joseph Viti, for patience, humor, and inspiring poses; you were the perfect Hector stand-in.

Thanks also to Orenna Krut, for thoughtful reading; archivists Gabriele Mohale and Zofia Sulej at the University of the Witwatersrand Historical Papers Research Archive, Johannesburg; the archivists at the National Library of South Africa (Pretoria); and the Society of Children's Book Writers and Illustrators.

I am most fortunate to have a wonderful publisher, Kristen Nobles, and to work with the Page Street Kids team, especially designer Melia Parsloe and dream editor Charlotte Wenger. Thank you all.

Selected Sources

"16 June 1976: The Day Hector Pieterson Died." Brand South Africa. June 15, 2004. https://www. brandsouthafrica.com/south-africa-fast-facts/history-facts/16-june-1976-day-hector-pieterson-died.

"Apartheid and Reactions to It." *South African History Online*. March 21, 2011. Last updated August 10, 2017. https://www.sahistory.org.za/article/apartheid-and-reactions-it.

Baker, Aryn. "This Photo Galvanized the World Against Apartheid. Here's the Story Behind It." *Time* online. June 15, 2016. http://time.com/4365138/soweto-anniversary-photograph.

"Bantu Education and the Racist Compartmentalizing of Education." *South African History Online*. March 30, 2011. Last updated June 10, 2016. https://www.sahistory.org.za/article/bantu-education-and-racist-compartmentalizing-education.

Bonner, Philip, and Lauren Segal. *Soweto, A History*. Cape Town: Maskew Miller Longman (Pty) Ltd, 1998.

Cartillier, Jerome. "How One Photograph Changed the World." Mail & Guardian. June 15, 2006. https://mg.co .za/article/2006-06-15-how-one-photograph-changed-the-world.

"A History of Apartheid in South Africa." *South African History Online*. May 6, 2016. Last updated March 15, 2018. https://www.sahistory.org.za/article/history-apartheid-south-africa.

"The June 16 Soweto Youth Uprising." *South African History Online*. May 21, 2013. Last updated May 21, 2018. https://www.sahistory.org.za/topic/june-16-soweto-youth-uprising.

Lines, Andy. "Nelson Mandela Remembered: The Tragic Mother Who Became Madiba's Hero." *Mirror* online. Last updated December 9, 2013. https://www.mirror.co.uk/news/world-news/nelson-mandela -remembered-tragic-mother-2907010.

Molosankwe, Botho. "Hector Pieterson Pic Ruined My Life." *Independent* online. June 12, 2013. https://www. iol.co.za/news/south-africa/gauteng/hector-pieterson-pic-ruined-my-life-1531027.

"National Anthem." South African Consulate General, New York City. http://www.southafrica-newyork.net /consulate/anthem.html.

"Through The Cracks: The untold story of Mbuyisa Makhubu." Eyewitness News. http://ewn.co.za/features /mbuyisa/.